ASTRID BERGMAN SUCKSDORFF

Tooni
The Elephant Boy

HARCOURT BRACE JOVANOVICH, INC.

NEW YORK

by the same author

CHENDRU: The Boy and the Tiger

THE ROE DEER

First American edition, 1971

Hardbound edition ISBN 0-15-289426-8

Library edition ISBN 0-15-289427-6

Library of Congress Catalog Card Number: 73-137762

Layout by Herbert Lindgren

Produced by International Book Production

Printed in Hong Kong

This is Tooni.
He is nine
years old and
lives in Assam,
a part of
India.

Beyond Tooni's village, beside the great Brahmaputra River, is the Kaziranga Game Sanctuary, a large area where all animals are protected. The sanctuary, which is thirty miles long and twelve miles wide, includes swamps, dense jungle, and open plains covered with tall grass.

In Tooni's village, many families live together in the same house. Tooni's father, whose name is Kone, works in the sanctuary as a mahout, which is what an elephant driver is called. In fact, all the men in the village are mahouts and work on the government-owned land with elephants that are the property of the Indian Forests Department. Tooni's mother is called Aiti, and his two-year-old brother's name is Radyo.

Each morning at sunrise Aiti sweeps in front of the house before going down to the river to fetch water for tea. Kone goes off to Joytara, a forty-year-old cow-elephant who is tethered a little way from the house. Although Joytara belongs to the Forests Department, Tooni's father thinks of her as his own.

Tooni usually helps his father to saddle Joytara before he goes to school.

Part of Kone's job is to protect the sanctuary from game
poachers and to take people to see the wild animals. Some-
times a class from an Assam school goes out with their
teacher. Early in the morning and late in the afternoon,
when the animals are feeding, are the best times to see them.
They rest during the worst heat in the middle of the day.

Visitors come to the Kazir-anga Sanctuary from many countries, especially to see the Indian rhinoceroses, the largest rhinos in the world. They can weigh as much as two tons and grow to a height of more than six feet, and they are extremely dangerous if approached too closely. The horn on their snouts is made of flesh, not bone, and if one is knocked off, a new one appears. These horns are as precious as gold, for they are used to make medicine that people in India believe will make weak men strong.

Tooni and his best friends, Dipa and Pradip, always walk to school together beside the river.

Inside the schoolhouse, children sit on the floor in different groups.

Pradip has done his sums correctly, but Tooni has made a mistake on his slate.

When Tooni comes home from school, he has some tea and boiled rice, and then it is time to go into the forest with his father for elephant food.

Tooni and Kone ride together on Joytara through a big tea plantation where the tea bushes have been recently pruned to improve their growth next season. Kone's brother, Rabilal, usually goes with them on Saraswati, an elephant calf who is only three years old.

When they come to
dense jungle, there is
plenty of foliage to cut
for elephant fodder.

Kone slashes with his sharp knife,
and Joytara passes up to him long
branches that she has broken off
with her trunk. Tooni helps Rabilal
to load Saraswati.

Every day they must bring back
great loads of green fodder.

When they have unloaded the leaves and branches back in the village, Tooni and his father go down to the river to give Joytara her daily bath. She lies down in the water while Tooni and Kone scrub her with handfuls of dry grass.

Joytara enjoys her bath, but little Radyo cries when Aiti tries to wash him.

Tooni knows exactly how a mahout gets up onto an elephant. First he says "*Khul*," which means "Ears forward." Then he gets hold of both Joytara's ears, places one foot on her trunk, and says "*Dele*," which means "Lift up." Joytara raises her trunk so that Tooni can climb up to the top of her head.

Kone guides the elephant by pressing with his bare feet, in different ways, behind Joytara's huge ears, and he uses special words that she understands. "*Aget*" means "Go forward." "*Pishu*" means "Go backward." "*Baith*" means "Lie down." Kone, like the other mahouts, carries a small hooked goad called an *ankosh*. This is used only if Joytara disobeys. Then he prods with it behind one of her ears.

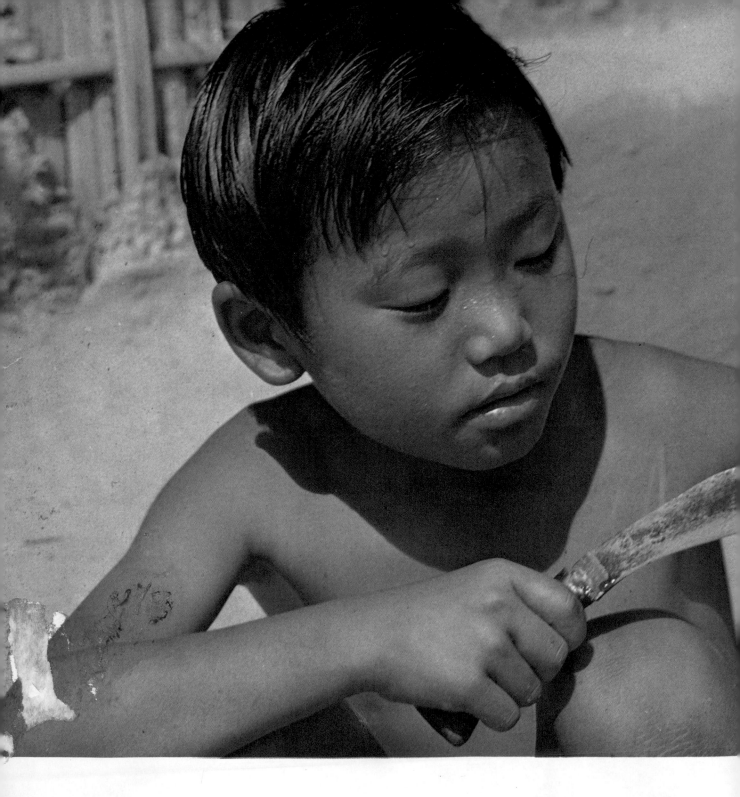

One evening, when they were sharpening their wood-
chopping knives, Kone said, "Tooni, you may come with
me into the sanctuary tomorrow. If we're lucky, we may see
a herd of wild elephants." Tooni was excited, Aiti was
pleased, but Radyo just seemed to wonder what was
happening.

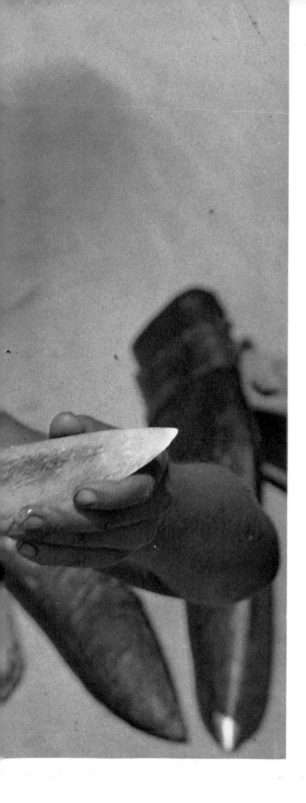

Long ago Joytara had been one of a big herd of wild elephants in the jungle. As they rode along the next day, Kone explained how wild elephants are caught. First a round enclosure called a *khedda* is made with strong saplings. After the wild elephants have been rounded up, they are driven through an opening into the khedda where the mahouts tie up each wild elephant to a tamed one, an extremely dangerous and difficult task. Then the elephants are brought out pair by pair.

"Because Joytara was quick to learn, it took only six months to train her to become an obedient working elephant," Kone told Tooni as they rode on.

Near the river they noticed a tiger's spoor, still fresh, and suddenly a huge tiger slipped by, all golden and splendid. "How beautiful he is," whispered Tooni.

"There are a lot of tigers here in Kaziranga," said Kone, "but they are never short of food because there are so many deer in the sanctuary. That's why it's seldom dangerous for men here."

On the far side of the river there was a big grassy plain where a herd of buffaloes were grazing. "They are shy, cautious creatures," said Kone, "but if they have to protect their young, full-grown buffaloes will charge without hesitation. Even a tiger will not face an angry buffalo. The buffaloes like to graze near water holes and muddy pools where they can wallow and cool themselves."

Tooni spotted a wild boar and a heron nearby. Cow-herons, as they are often called, perch on the backs of buffaloes and peck at the insects they find there.

After Tooni and his father crossed the wide plain, they came to water and saw a flock of birds in a big tree. There were storks with long legs and beaks, herons, and young pelicans whose feathers had not yet turned white. "The birds are watching the shallow water below for fish, frogs, lizards, and insects," said Kone.

Tooni pointed to a big cloud of smoke in the distance,
billowing into the sky. Every year the long grass is burned
off so that good new grass will grow for the wild animals to
graze on.

"Look," said Tooni, seeing something in the water.
"What's that dark lump?" And as they came nearer, a large
rhinoceros clambered onto the bank.

A herd of swamp deer raced quickly away as Kone and
Tooni rode up. "They're *barasingha* or big horns," Kone
said. "Their hoofs are broad so they can run over swampy
ground without sinking in."

And a little farther on they came upon four rhinoceroses. "A rare sight," as Kone told Tooni, "because there are only about seven hundred one-horned rhinos left in the world. Most of them are in India, but there are a few in Nepal. Africa has its rhinos, too, but they're a different species with two horns on the nose instead of one."

It was time to start for home. As Joytara turned, Tooni
spotted something on the ground, and Kone guided Joytara
over to it. "*Mele, mele*," Kone commanded Joytara, and she
felt with her trunk along the ground until it closed on a
dark object that she lifted and handed to Kone. "Tooni! It's
a rhinoceros horn! Two male rhinos probably had a fight
and one has lost this horn. We must take it to the Forestry
Officer at once – he'll be excited, too."

When Tooni and his father proudly presented their find to the Forestry Officer, he told Tooni, "There'll be a reward for this. It is worth many thousand rupees – enough probably to buy a new working elephant."

Tooni grinned with pleasure.

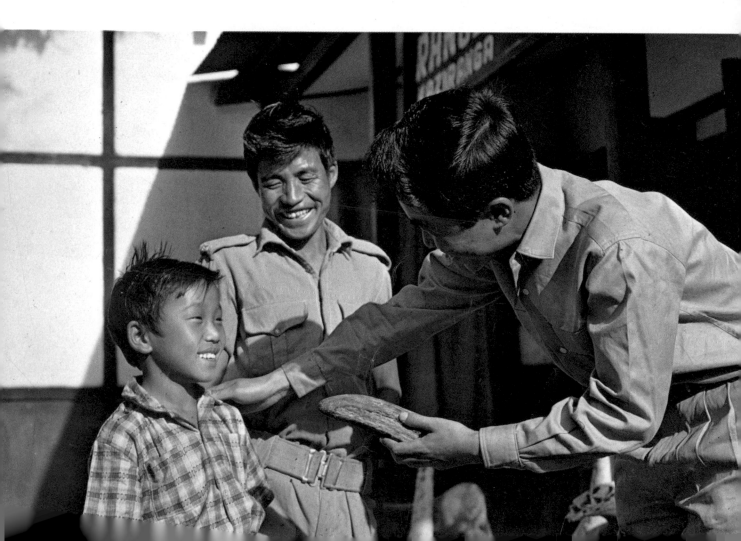

Night had fallen. The sun had gone down behind the mountains, and Joytara was munching away outside the mahouts' house. Aiti, Kone, and little Radyo were all asleep.

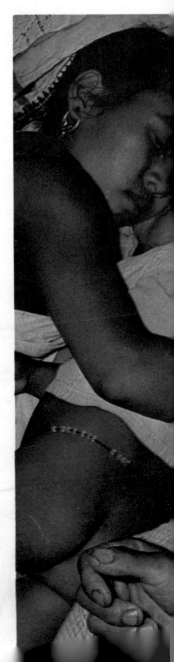

Tooni, too, was asleep, but he was dreaming of a big,
big elephant – the most beautiful elephant in the whole
world with long white tusks and the most splendid name he
could think of: Akbar! That was what the elephant would
be called, and Tooni would be his mahout.

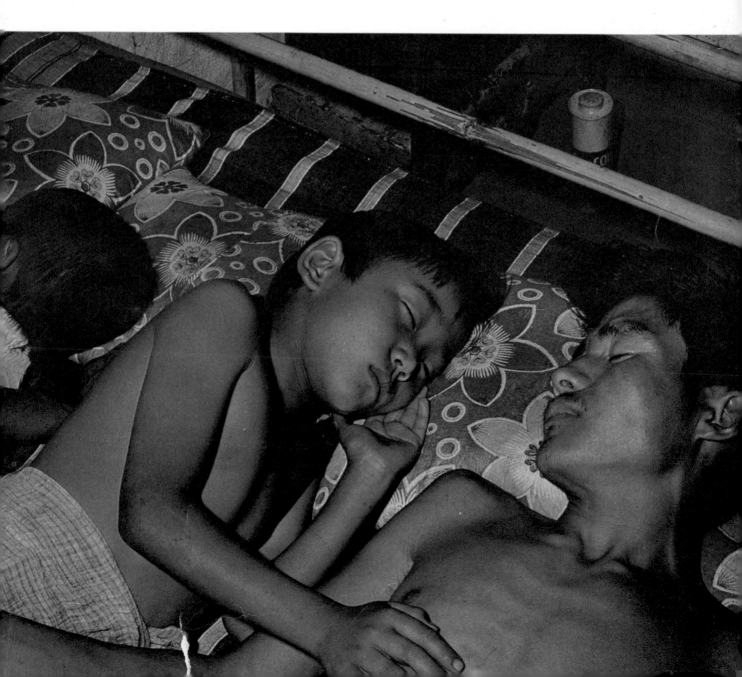